ALAN KATZ PRESENTS

THE FUNNIEST JOKE BOOK EVER FOR KIDS

SCHOLASTIC INC.

ISBN 978-93-5954-562-2

First printing 2024
This reprint edition March 2026
Book design by Ellen Duda
Chicken photo credit © Shutterstock
Illustrations by Ellen Duda

Printed in India at Shivam Offset Press, New Delhi

To everyone who's ever told me a joke

A Letter from Alan Katz

Hello, dear reader!

(I'm calling you that because, honestly, I don't know your name. But *you* probably do.)

My name is Alan Katz, and my job is to make people laugh. I've done that in a whole bunch of humorous books for kids, including picture books, songbooks, chapter books, poetry collections, and more. I've also done it by writing stage shows, episodes of animated and live-action TV series, and radio programs. I've even written jokes for famous comedians.

Other people are great at fixing teeth, flying airplanes, inventing important medical devices, and being teachers and librarians (oh boy, do I love teachers and librarians!). But my entire career has been based on thinking up things that'll make people laugh.

It's a very cool job. I love it a lot. I also love tomato soup a lot, but that's not important right now.

What *is* important is what I'm about to say.

While I hope this book makes you laugh until your head falls off, once you put your head back on, I hope you'll remember this:

Being funny is wonderful. But it is never, never, never okay to make a joke that hurts anyone's feelings. It's not okay to make fun of another person's backpack, or how they throw a ball, or what they're having for lunch, or their name, or anything like that. I don't care if ten million people are laughing at a joke; if the joke you say (or write) hurts even one person's feelings, it's not a joke that should ever be told.

Being funny feels great. But being *kind* feels waaaaaaaay better!

So be funny sometimes. But *always, always* be kind.

Got it? Great. Let's get ready to laugh.

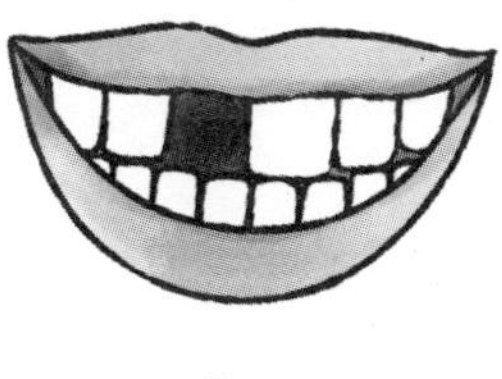

SOME CHILLY SILLY RIDDLES

What did the snowman's mother say when they left for school?

"Have an ice day!"

How do polar bears make their beds?

With sheets of ice and blankets of snow.

What do they sing at Frosty's birthday party?

Freeze a Jolly Good Fellow!

What kind of ball doesn't bounce?

A snowball!

What's a snowman's favorite drink?

Iced tea.

Where's a good place to check the weather forecast in January?

The winter-net.

Why was the snowman sorting through a bag of carrots?

He wanted to pick his nose.

What do you call an old snowman?

Water.

Doctors and Ha-Ha-Hospitals

A child walked into a doctor's office and said, "Every time I drink hot chocolate, I get a sharp pain in my eye."
The doctor said, "Next time, take the spoon out before you sip."

Why did the banana go to the doctor?
It wasn't peeling good.

Hayden: Guess who I bumped into on the way to the eye doctor today.
Aisha: Who?
Hayden: Everyone! I need glasses!

Why did the pie go to the dentist?
It needed a filling.

Jamie: Dr. Smith, guess what—
I can see into the future!

Dr. Smith: How long have you been able to do that?

Jamie: Since next Thursday!

A child went to the emergency room doctor and said, "Help me—I just coughed up a knight, a bishop, and a pawn."
The doctor said, "Sounds like you have a chess infection."

Why are doctors who treat babies usually so short-tempered?
Because they have very little patients.

A child went to the doctor and said, "Doctor, doctor. I think I'm a dog."
The doctor said, "I can't help you—you should go see a vet."

A Good Number of Number Jokes

If you had 13 apples, 12 grapes, 3 pineapples, and 3 strawberries, what would you have?

A delicious fruit salad.

What did 0 say to 8?

Nice belt!

Alijah: I'm very quick at math.

Valerie: Oh yeah? How much is 25 times 28?

Alijah: 19.

Valerie: That's not even close to correct.

Alijah: I didn't say I was correct. I said I was quick.

Which king loved fractions?

Henry the Eighth.

Are monsters good at math?

Not unless you Count Dracula.

What are 10 things you can always count on?

Your fingers!

Milton: Did you hear—the numbers 19 and 20 got into a fight!

Samantha: What happened?

Milton: 21.

Kevin: My cousin invented the number zero.

Carol: Tell them thanks for nothing.

Animal Jokes to Drive You Wild

What did the buffalo say when his male child left for camp?

Bison!

How do bees get to school?

They take the buzz.

What's orange and sounds like a parrot?

A carrot!

What do you call a deer with no eyes?

No-eye-deer.

What goes "tick, *woof*, tick, *woof*"?

A watch dog.

What's a frog's favorite drink?

Croak-a-Cola.

What is a cow's favorite holiday?

Moo Year's Day!

Why do you never see pigs hiding in trees?

Because they're very good at it!

A child walks into a pet store and asks for a dozen bees.

The shop owner counts out 13 bees and hands them to the child.

"Wait, that's one too many!" the child says.

"It's a freebie," the owner says.

Why did the chicken cross the playground?

To get to the other slide.

What do you say to a rabbit 365 days after it was born?

Hoppy birthday!

What do you sing to a cat on its birthday?

Happy Birthday to Mew.

Which is the loudest pet of all?

A trumpet!

What sound do porcupines make when they kiss?

Ouch!

What kind of dog loves taking bubble baths?

A shampoodle!

What's the difference between elephants and grapes?

Grapes are purple.

What school subject do snakes like best?

Hissssstory!

What does a rancher use to keep track of his cattle?

A cow-culator!

Why shouldn't you tell a pig a secret?

Because they always end up squealing.

What insect smells the best?

A deodor-ant.

Why don't they play board games in the jungle?

Too many cheetahs.

What do you call a Chihuahua in July?

A hot dog.

What do you call two birds in love?

Tweethearts!

What do you call a funny chicken?

A comedi-hen.

TRY NOT TO LOL CHALLENGE

I hope this book has made you giggle, chuckle, guffaw, and shake with laughter.

But for the next bunch of jokes, let's try something different: I challenge you to read the jokes and try not to laugh. See how many jokes in a row you can read without LoLing.

Then read them to others and see if they can hold back the laughter.

Each time you make someone laugh, you get one point. But each time they don't LoL, they get a point.

Keep score, and see who gets to 10 points first. Or you could also tally up who gets more points in 5 minutes. Or see who gets more points in 11 years, 9 months, 6 days, 3 hours, 14 minutes, and 27 seconds.

Did you just laugh at that?

One point for me!

Have fun . . . but remember: Try not to LoL!

I asked my friend to tell me when their birthday was.

They said, "March first."

So I stomped around the room, but they still wouldn't tell me.

Lenyn: What rhymes with orange.

Teddy: No, it doesn't.

Noah: Why was the clock asked to leave the library?

Emily: It was tocking too loudly.

Why was the broom late for work?

It over-swept!

What always comes at the end of Thanksgiving?

The letter *g*.

What's red and smells like blue paint?

Red paint.

Why didn't the teddy bear eat dessert?

Because it was already stuffed.

What happens when a grape gets run over while crossing the street?

Traffic jam!

What's red and bad for your teeth?

A brick.

How does the ocean say hi?

It waves.

Raph: I can cut a piece of wood in half just by looking at it.

Donnie: That's not true!

Raph: Yes it is—I saw it with my own eyes!

Dave: My brother was injured in a peekaboo accident.

Alan: What did you do?

Dave: I took him to the ICU.

Okay, the "Try Not to LoL" jokes are done. For now—there'll be a lot more later on in the book. It's perfectly fine to laugh again . . . until further notice!!!

Prank You Very Much

Here's a safe and silly prank you can try on a friend or family member:

The next time you see someone eating cotton candy, tell them it's important to wash it before eating. Give them a small bowl of water and have them drop in a piece of the cotton candy. It'll dissolve instantly! Then say, "Um, maybe I was thinking of apples. You're supposed to wash apples before you eat them. Sorry!"

Read These to Your Anagram-ma

It's fun to rearrange letters in words and phrases . . . that's called making anagrams. And sometimes when you do, you end up with another really funny word or phrase. Here are some that are pretty hilarious . . .

Rearrange the letters in THE EYES, and you get THEY SEE.

Rearrange the letters in ELEVEN PLUS TWO, and you get TWELVE PLUS ONE.

Rearrange the letters in MORSE CODE, and you get HERE COME DOTS.

Rearrange the letters in LISTEN, and you get SILENT.

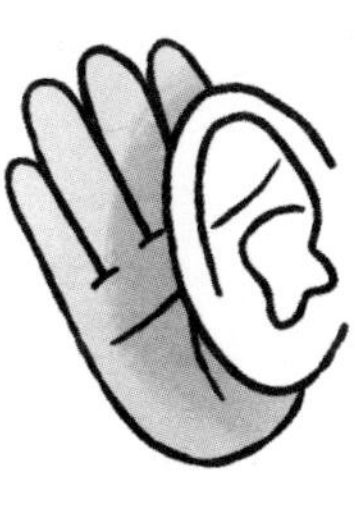

The (Holiday) Gift of Laughter

Ross: My holiday gift is unbeatable!

Tina: What did you get?

Ross: A broken drum.

Where's a good place to look for gifts for a kitty?

In a cat-alog.

It's better to give than to receive.
That's a simple fact I truly believe.
So to spread much good cheer
at this time of the year,
I'll give you a list of what I want to receive.

Where do werewolves purchase holiday gifts?

Beast Buy.

James: Thanks for the present. But why did you give me a frog?

Seth: I want to wish you hoppy holidays!

Would you like this box of wet winter precipitation?

Snow thank you.

What do holiday gifts enjoy listening to on the radio?

Wrap music!

Marcus: Why did you give me salt and pepper for the holidays?

L.J.: It's my way of saying "seasonings greetings!"

HAVE A BALL WITH THESE SPORTS JOKES

Why are basketball courts always wet?

Because the players dribble.

What can be served but never eaten?

A volleyball.

What is a boxer's favorite drink?

Punch.

Why is Cinderella so bad at soccer?

Because she always runs away from the ball.

What do sprinters eat before a race?

Nothing. They fast.

What kind of race is never run?

A swim race.

What's a swimmer's favorite math subject?

Dive-ision.

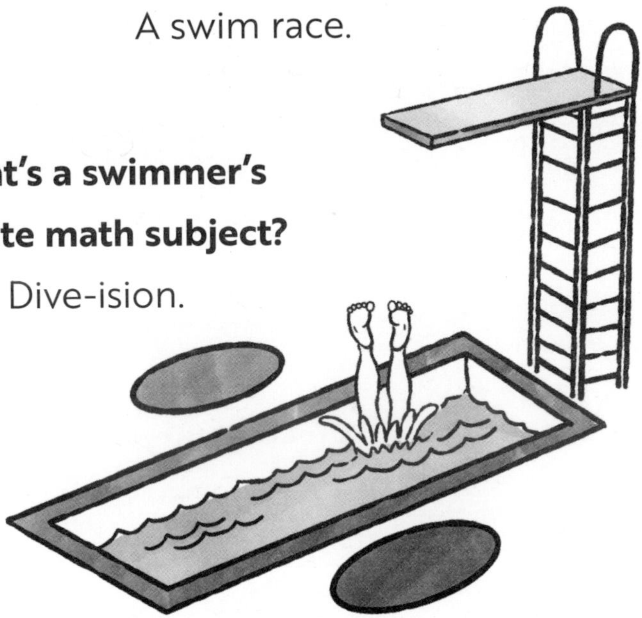

What did the football coach say to the broken vending machine?

I want my quarter back.

Boo to You!

Why do witches ride broomsticks?

Because vacuum cleaners are too heavy to fly.

When is a pumpkin not a pumpkin?

When you drop it—then it's squash.

What is a witch's favorite subject in school?

Spelling!

How do you fix a cracked jack-o'-lantern?

You use a pumpkin patch!

Why didn't the skeleton go to the dance?

It had no body to dance with.

What's the best thing to put in a pumpkin pie?

Your teeth.

What position does a ghost play in soccer?

Ghoulie!

What is a skeleton's favorite instrument?

The trombone!

Thanksgiving Thanks-for-Laughing!

If you serve a rubber turkey, what day is it?

Pranksgiving!

Why do turkeys make bad baseball players?

They only hit fowl balls!

What's a turkey's favorite dessert?

Peach gobbler!

Why was the turkey asked to join the band?

Because they can bring their own drumsticks.

Family Starts with *F* . . . And So Does Funny!

Sara: My cousin said they drove past an apple pie, a piece of cake, and an ice cream sundae in the road.

Dave: Sounds like the streets were desserted.

My little brother was asked to write a 100-word essay. He wrote: My cat ran outside, so I went and called him. "Here kitty, kitty!"

My father got fired from the calendar factory. All he did was take a day off.

Savannah: Is it true that your uncle is a good magician?

Brielle: He sure is—yesterday he was walking down the street and he turned into a bookstore!

TRY NOT TO LOL CHALLENGE

Remember back on page 18, I asked you to try not to LoL at some jokes? I really hope you remember that, and I really, really hope you were able to do it. Now I really, really hope you're ready to do it again. Really!

Susan: Want to hear the joke about the tissue paper?

Julia: No, it's probably tearable.

What do Alexander the Great and Winnie the Pooh have in common?

Same middle name.

What's a king's favorite kind of weather?

Reign.

Why couldn't the bicycle stand on its own?

It was two-tired.

What did the traffic light say to the truck?

Don't look, I'm changing.

What's blue and not heavy?

Light blue.

What can you put in your right hand but not in your left hand?

Your left elbow.

How do you make the number one disappear?

By adding the letter *g*. Then it's "gone."

What five-letter word becomes shorter after you add two letters?

Short (add the *e-r*).

What has one head, one foot, and four legs?

A bed.

What's red and moves up and down?

A tomato in an elevator.

What do you get if you cross a pie and a snake?

A pie-thon!

PRANK YOU VERY MUCH

Take two different kinds of breakfast cereals from the cupboard and switch the bags. Then wait as an adult pours themselves a bowl of sugary flakes meant for kids . . . and kids pour themselves a bowl of boring adult cereal. Watch it happen, but if you're gonna laugh, laugh quietly.

One Word Says It All

Puns are often formed by using words that have more than one meaning. For example, the joke "Why shouldn't you trust trees? They seem shady." It's funny because trees are shady, because they provide shade. But the word shady *has another meaning—not being trustworthy. Get it? Are you LoLing . . . or managing to hold back the laugh?*

Either way, here's a challenge to see if you can figure out which word applies to both meanings. Do it well, and you just might be able to create your own puns.

There's one in a car, and there's one on a steer.

____

It's a word that's used if someone's afraid,
and it's also something that crosses the road.

____

You've got one in your mouth,
and you've got one in your shoe.

____

There's one on the mound, and there's
also one on the table filled with water.

____

ANSWERS: HORN CHICKEN TONGUE PITCHER

Don't Laugh with Your Mouth Full!

What did the banana say to the ostrich?

Nothing. Bananas can't talk.

What kind of fruit can fix your sink?

A plum-ber.

Why do some people eat snails?

They don't enjoy fast food.

What does a nut say when it sneezes?

Cashew!

What kind of vegetable likes to look at animals?

A zoo-chini!

What is a zucchini's favorite game?

Squash!

How many apples grow on a tree?

All of them!

Victor: My friend Jack says he can communicate with vegetables.

Reed: Really?

Victor: Yes, Jack and the beans talk.

Why shouldn't you tell a burrito a secret?

They might end up spilling the beans.

What do an apple and an orange have in common?

Neither one can drive.

What do you call a potato with no feet?

A potato.

Have you heard the rumor about butter?

Never mind, I shouldn't be spreading it.

Fiona: Why did you smear peanut butter on the road?

Margot: It will go well with the traffic jam!

When do you go at red and stop at green?

When you're eating a watermelon.

Where did spaghetti and sauce go to dance?

The meat ball.

What is one thing you can never have for lunch or dinner?

Breakfast.

Jokes About School? How Very Cool!

Why did the teacher put on sunglasses?

Because their students were very bright!

Why shouldn't you write with a broken pencil?

Because it's pointless.

Why is a math book always unhappy?

Because it has a lot of problems.

How did the beauty school student do on their manicure test?

They nailed it!

Why did the music teacher bring a ladder to school?

They wanted to reach the high notes!

What should you do if your teacher rolls their eyes at you?

Pick them up and roll them back.

What's a teacher's favorite nation?

An expla-nation.

What do librarians use as bait when they want to catch fish?

Bookworms!

Mike: Why do magicians do so well in school?

Leo: I don't know. Why?

Mike: They're good at trick questions.

Name the only word in the dictionary that's spelled wrong.

Wrong.

Yesenia: I just read a book about helium.

Brittny: Was it any good?

Yesenia: I couldn't put it down.

What did the janitor yell when they jumped out of the closet?

"Supplies!"

Serena: Hey, Mom, I got a hundred in school today!

Mom: That's great!

Serena: Not really; I got a 40 in reading and a 60 in spelling.

Teacher: Why is your homework in your parent's handwriting?

Student: I used their pen.

Why did the student eat their homework?

Because the teacher said the assignment was a piece of cake.

Who is the king of the school supplies?

The ruler!

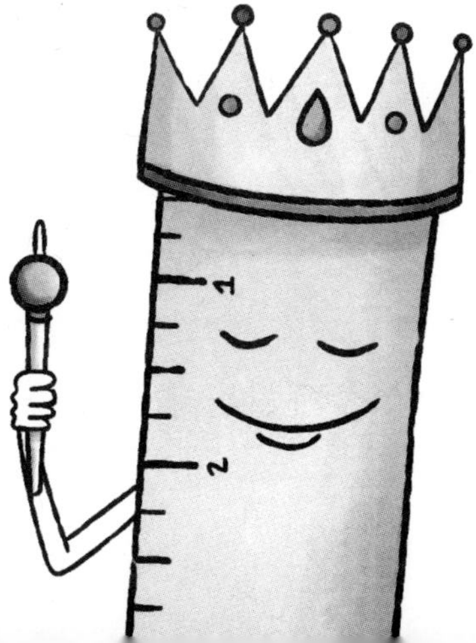

REMEMBER THE ANIMALS? THEY'RE BACK . . . WITH A JOKE ATTACK!

Why don't lobsters like to share?

They're shellfish.

What do you call a bee that can't make up its mind?

A may-bee.

How does a penguin build its house?

Igloos it.

Have you heard the joke about the skunk?

Never mind, it really stinks.

What kind of insects enjoy reading the dictionary?

Spelling bees!

What is a cat's favorite color?

Purr-ple.

Why are elephants so wrinkled?

You ever try to iron one?

What do you call the horse that lives next door?

Your neigh-bor.

1 + 1 = Fun (Math and Science Laughs)

How does a scientist freshen their breath?

With experi-mints!

How do you stop an astronaut's baby from crying?

You rocket!

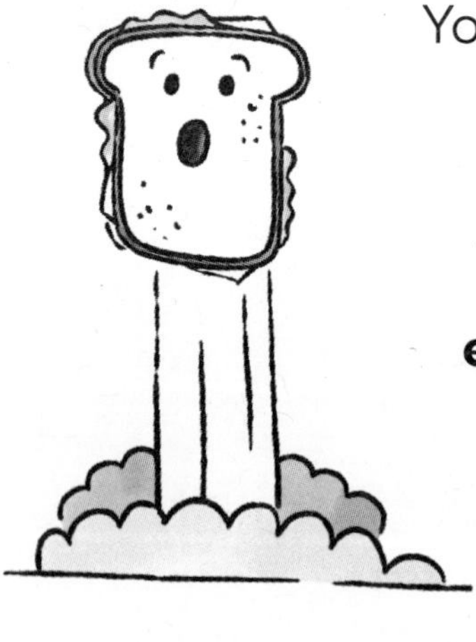

When do astronauts eat their sandwiches?

At launchtime!

Why did the scientist wear denim?

Because they are a jean-ius.

Anthony: Is it true you let that spider use your computer?

Amad: Yes, it wanted to make a website.

What tool do mathematicians use most?

Multi-pliers.

Which is faster, hot or cold?

Hot, because you can catch cold.

What kind of music do planets like?

Nep-tunes.

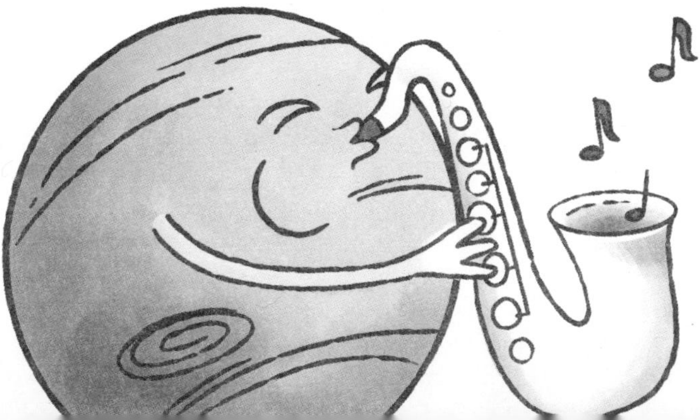

Try Not to LoL Challenge

Many cities have electronic signs that alternate between "Walk" and "Don't Walk"—they tell you when it's safe to cross the street. This book, however, doesn't have that kind of light-up message. If it did, it would be flashing "Don't Laugh" for the next three pages.

Got it? Have fun . . . but try not to LoL!

What do you call a bear with no teeth?

A gummy bear!

What kind of sports cars do cats drive?

Fur-arris.

What do a tick and the Eiffel Tower have in common?

They're both Paris sites.

What do you get if you cross a sheepdog with a rose?

A collie flower.

Why didn't the sun go to college?

It already had a million degrees.

What is a tree's least favorite month?

Sep-timber.

What kind of music does a boulder enjoy?

Rock 'n' roll.

What does the garden ornament do after school?

Its gnomework.

Which animal is best at sports?

A score-pion.

Natalie: Was the lamp happy when you turned it off?

Sol: Happy? It was de-lighted!

What does a nosy pepper do?

It gets jalapeño business.

What's an astronaut's favorite key on a keyboard?

The space bar.

Prank You Very Much

Ask a friend to sit down and then move their right leg in a continuous clockwise circle. Then tell them you can make their leg change directions without touching them. They'll probably say, "No, you can't." But you can . . . and here's how. While they're making the continuous clockwise circles with their right leg, tell them to use their right hand to make a giant number six in the air. When they do, their leg will change direction and go counterclockwise. Seems unbelievable, but it works. Try it yourself, and then challenge your friends to do it!

FACTS, SCHMACTS!

I'll give you a word or phrase that rhymes with the correct answer. It's your job to figure out the real answer. Got it? Good. And wood duck. I mean . . . good luck!

What is the capital of Delaware? Rhyming answer: ROVER

Your answer: ______________________________

Name the vegetable that grows on a stalk and contains kernels. Rhyming answer: BORN ON THE BLOB

Your answer: ______________________________

In which city is LaGuardia Airport located?

Rhyming answer: CHEW FORK

Your answer: ______________________________

What kind of animal slithers? Rhyming answer: RAKE

Your answer: ______________________________

What's the name of the board game in which you form words with letter tiles? Rhyming answer: BABBLE

Your answer: ______________________________

ANSWERS: DOVER CORN ON THE COB NEW YORK SNAKE SCRABBLE

Tee-Hee-Hees About Tre-Tre-Trees

What kind of tree can you hold in your hand?

A palm tree!

Why did the tree go to the dentist?

It needed a root canal.

Where do young trees go to learn?

Elemen-tree school.

What did the beaver say to the tree?

It's been nice gnawing you.

A Handful of Jokes About Jokes

Lee: I thought you said you were going to tell me a construction joke.

Eliza: Sorry, I'm still working on it.

Pedro: Want to hear two short jokes and a long joke?

Jacob: Sure!

Pedro: Joke. Joke. Joooooooooooke!

Knock, knock.

Who's there?

Shore.

Shore who?

Shore hope you like this joke!

Why isn't it a good idea to tell a joke to an egg?

It might crack up!

There's No Place (to Laugh) Like Home

What runs but never goes anywhere?

A refrigerator.

Dylan: My dog shed all over the couch and chairs.

Al: Well, they *do* call it fur-niture!

What do you call a can opener that doesn't work?

A can't opener.

Isabella: My parents sold our vacuum cleaner the other day.

Gianna: Why?

Isabella: All it was doing was collecting dust.

What musical instrument might you find in your bathroom?

A tuba toothpaste.

What does a house wear?

Address.

Where does a rose sleep at night?

In a flower bed.

What kind of flower should you never give on Mother's Day?

Cauliflower.

WHAT IN THE WORLD?

Which state has a lot of cats and dogs?

Pets-ylvania.

Where do crayons go on vacation?

Color-ado.

Knock, knock.

Who's there?

Ida.

Ida who?

Sorry, you're wrong. It's pronounced Idaho.

Which state gets the best report card?

Alabama—it always has four As and one B.

What stays in the corner but can travel all over the world?

A stamp.

Which US state is famous for its very small soft drinks?

Minnesota.

What's the capital of Louisiana?

Capital *L*.

Knock, knock.

Who's there?

Europe.

Europe who?

No, you're a poo!

Try Not to LoL Challenge

For what seems like the 4,573rd time in this book, I'm gonna challenge you to read some jokes and not LoL. Why? Well, according to some possibly phony-baloney information on the internet, it takes more than twice as many muscles to frown as it does to smile. So . . . by not laughing, you're giving much-needed exercise to your frown muscles. Yes, don't LoL at the next bunch of jokes and you'll be doing a facial workout. Sort of. Technically. You're welcome. I think.

What do you call a rooster that's staring at a piece of lettuce?

Chicken sees a salad.

What do you call a fake noodle?

An impasta!

What did the police officer say to the belly button?

"You're under a vest!"

Why are art collectors such big fans of gasoline?

Because it can make their Van Gogh.

Why do pancakes always win in baseball?

Because they have the best batter.

Why do fish live in salt water?

Because pepper makes them sneeze.

What's gray and goes around and around?

An elephant in a washing machine.

What do you do if you see a spaceman?

Park your car, man.

What city is 3/7 chicken, 2/3 cat, and 2/4 goat?

Chi-ca-go.

What do you call a factory that makes products that are merely okay?

A satisfactory.

What's a cow's favorite drink?

A s-moooo-thie.

Michael: My dog is a genius.

Lucy: How do you know?

Michael: I asked it, "What's two minus two?" It said nothing.

Prank You Very Much

Get a piece of brown construction paper and write a block letter *E*. Then cut it out and hide it somewhere nearby. Next, ask a sibling (or a cousin, or a friend, or pretty much anyone you know) if they would like a brownie.

When they say yes, reach into your hiding place and pull out . . . the brown *E*.

For added fun, cut out many brown *E*s and put them on a tray. Next, announce to the family that you made a tray of brownies. Then wait for the fun when they see it's actually a tray full of brown *E*s.

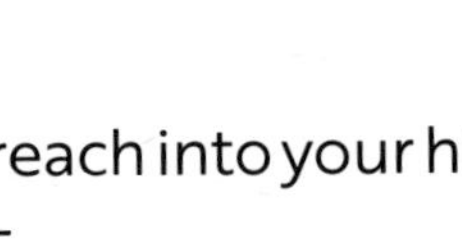

UNDER A SPELL

If you spell out numbers such as O-N-E, T-W-O, T-H-R-E-E, and so on . . . you don't use the letter *A* until you get to O-N-E T-H-O-U-S-A-N-D.

Speaking of spelling out the numbers, can you think of the only number that is spelled out with its letters in alphabetical order? This is a hard question, but one that is fun to challenge others with. And the answer is . . .

I'm not telling you. No matter how many times you ask me, I won't tell you. I don't care if you ask me forty times a day for forty days, I'm not telling you that the only number that's spelled out in alphabetical order is . . .

(Um, look above. It's F-O-R-T-Y.)

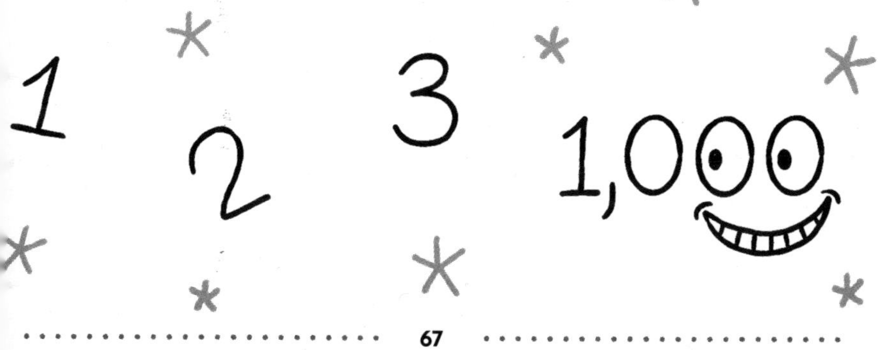

Some A-door-able Jokes

Knock, knock!

Who's there?

I-M.

I-M who?

I-M on the computer,
and I can't answer the door.

Knock, knock!

Who's there?

Cows go.

Cows go who?

No, silly, owls go *who.*

Cows go *moo*!

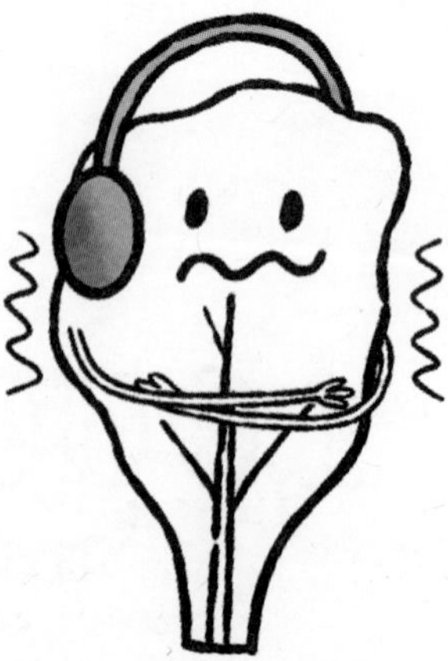

Knock, knock.

Who's there?

Lettuce.

Lettuce who?

Lettuce in, it's cold outside!

Knock, knock!

Who's there?

Harry.

Harry who?

Harry up and open the door!

Knock, knock!

Who's there?

Lena.

Lena who?

Lena little closer and I'll tell you!

Knock, knock!

Who's there?

Theodore.

Theodore who?

Theodore wasn't open so I knocked!

Knock, knock!

Who's there?

A pile-up.

A pile-up who?

Oh, that's disgusting!

Knock, knock!
Who's there?
Turnip
Turnip who?
Turnip the radio, please!

Knock, knock!
Who's there?
Wooden shoe.
Wooden shoe who?
Wooden shoe like to hear another joke?

Knock, knock!
Who's there?
Hike.
Hike who?
Oh, I didn't know you like Japanese poetry.

Knock, knock!
Who's there?
Figs.
Figs who?
Figs the doorbell, it's not working!

Knock, knock.

Who's there?

Nobel.

Nobel who?

Nobel . . . that's why I knocked!

Knock, knock.

Who's there?

Water.

Water who?

Water you asking so many questions for? Just let me in!

Knock, knock.

Who's there?

Joanna.

Joanna who?

Joanna build a snowman?

Knock, knock.

Who's there?

Hawaii.

Hawaii who?

I'm fine. Hawaii you?

Just a Bunch of Goofy Giggles

What was Ludwig van Beethoven's favorite fruit?

Ba-na-na-na!

When is the worst time to build a snowman?

Summertime.

Miranda: Do you know how many famous people were born on your birthday?

Zane: None. Only babies were born on my birthday.

Why is the Statue of Liberty standing in New York Harbor?

Because she can't sit down.

Zoe: Someone came to our front door asking for donations for a community swimming pool.

Dimitri: Did you give them anything?

Zoe: Yes—a glass of water.

How do cats like to bake cakes?

From scratch.

Daisy: Guess what—I just dropped a raw egg onto a concrete floor, and it didn't crack.

Casey: That's not surprising—it's very hard to crack a concrete floor.

Three people jump into the water, but only two come out with wet hair. Why?

The third person is bald.

Who, What, Where, When, Ha!

Who do musicians see when they want their pants hemmed quickly?

Taylor Swift.

What can you break simply by saying its name?

Silence.

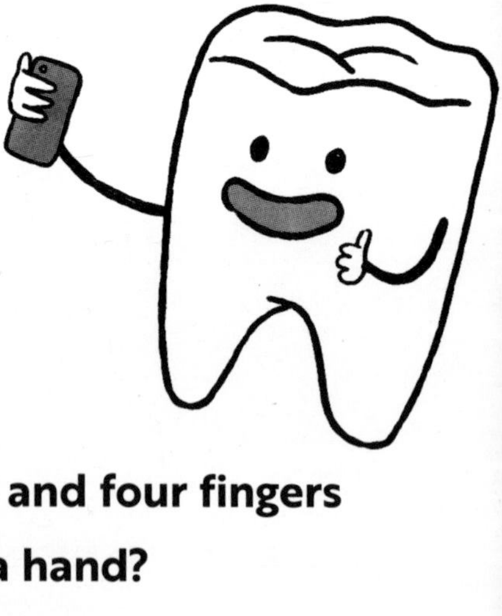

What do dentists call their X-rays?

Tooth pics!

What has a thumb and four fingers but isn't a hand?

A glove.

What looks just like half a loaf of bread?

The other half of that loaf of bread.

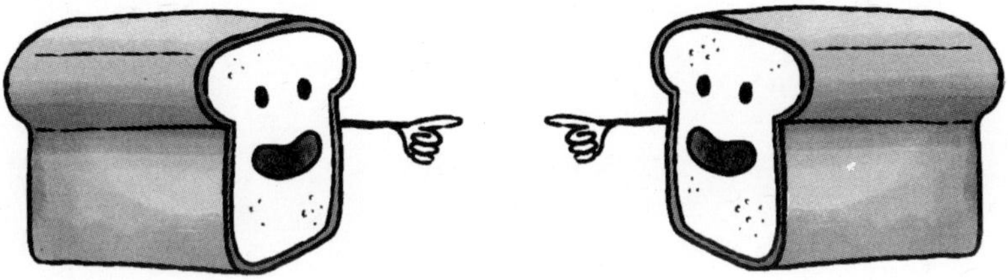

What goes up but never comes back down?

Your age.

What kind of tree grows words instead of leaves?

A poetry.

What gets larger the more you take away?

A hole in the ground.

JEST KIDDIN' AROUND

What do you call

a dog that floats?

Good buoy!

What has a head and a tail, but no body?

A coin.

Which kind of ship has two mates

but no captain?

Friendship.

Which football player has to wear

the largest helmet?

The one with the largest head.

What age can you eat for breakfast?

Saus-age.

Jade: I dropped a glass that was full and didn't spill a drop of milk.

Marisa: How is that possible?

Jade: The glass was full of water!

What has to be broken before you can use it?

An egg.

What did the potato chip say to the other potato chips?

"Shall we go for a dip?"

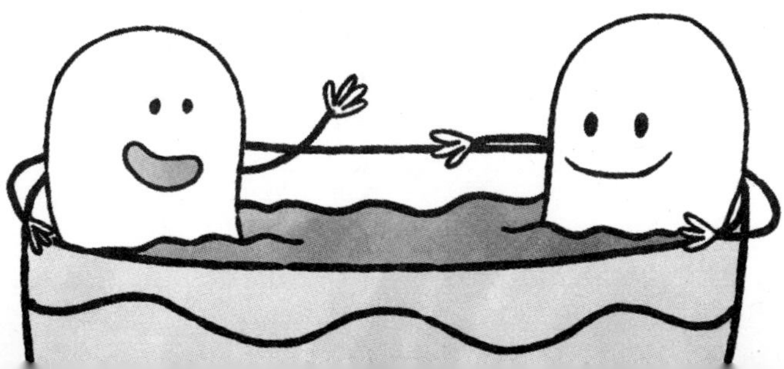

TRY NOT TO LOL CHALLENGE

Did you know that there's a person in Duluth, Minnesota, who has never laughed or smiled once? No matter how hilarious the joke or pun, they absolutely refuse to react as if something is funny. Okay, I totally made that up; there's no such person. But if there were someone like them, they'd appreciate (but not laugh at) the next twelve jokes. I hope you do the same.

Why can't humans hear a dog whistle?

Because dogs can't whistle!

Why are people so tired on April first?

Because they just finished a March that lasted 31 days.

How many cats can you put in an empty box?

Only one. After that, the box isn't empty!

Why are fish so easy to weigh?

Because they bring their own set of scales.

If athletes get athlete's foot, what do astronauts get?

Missile toe.

Why did the nose feel sad?

It was always getting picked on.

Where do baby cats learn to swim?

In the kitty pool.

What kind of bug is good at telling time?

A clock-roach.

What's the best way to raise a young dinosaur?

With a crane.

Paul: Do you know the difference between a bathroom and a kitchen?

Roman: No, I don't.

Paul: In that case, you're never going to be invited to my house.

What kind of music should you listen to while fishing?

Something catchy!

What did one elevator say to the other elevator?

I think I'm coming down with something.

Prank You Very Much

Pranks are fun when the pranker can watch the prank-ee in action. Here's a prank that's safe and enjoyable, but you won't be able to watch it happen—because the person you're pranking will be behind a closed door.

It's simple. Write a short message like "Smile for the camera!" or "Don't forget to wash your hands!" Then roll down (but don't rip off) a few sheets of toilet tissue, insert your note, and roll the paper back up.

When a family member uses the bathroom, they're sure to see your note when they unroll the toilet tissue to use it.

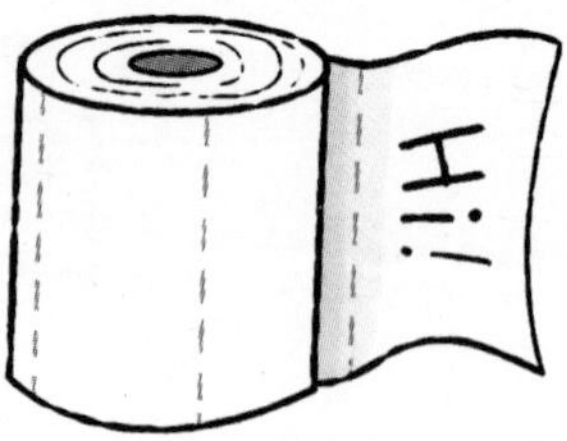

Po-ho-ho-etry

I can play harmonica.
I can play trombone.
I can play the clarinet.
Also, saxophone.
I can play the harp and flute.
But my folks complain when I'm
playing on those instruments
at the exact same time.

I can't drive a dump truck.
I can't drive a van.
I can't drive a subway train
or a catamaran.
I can't drive a tractor,
a limo, or a car.
But I can drive my parents nuts,
and that gets me really far.

Jokes They Enjoy in Pun-sylvania

What's a tornado's favorite game?

Twister.

If you get hungry at the beach and didn't bring any food, what can you do?

Eat all the sand which is there.

Which of the fifty US states sounds like it's the cleanest?

Washington.

What can be served but is never eaten?

A tennis ball.

What kind of tree is a ghost's favorite?

Bam-BOO!

Teacher: Ralph, why are you doing your multiplication on the floor?

Ralph: You told me to do it without using tables!

What letter of the alphabet is a question?

Y.

Which vegetable does a plumber dislike?

Leeks.

What has three feet but can't run?

A yardstick.

What do you call people who really love ceilings?

Ceiling fans.

What goes really fast and tastes great with salsa?

A rocket chip.

Which side of a turkey has the most feathers?

The outside.

What tastes better than it smells?

Your tongue.

What's green and fuzzy and would make a lot of noise if it fell out of a tree?

A pool table.

What do you call it when wooden cubes are having a neighborhood gathering?

A block party!

Why should you always knock on a refrigerator door before opening it?

In case there's a salad dressing.

SOME QUICK HIGH-QUALITY QUIPS!

What do you call a cow that's been knighted?

Sir Loin.

What do a pig and ink have in common?

You'll find them both in a pen.

Why would a giraffe be likely to drink more water in January than in February?

Because there are more days in January.

How did the pig get to the hospital?

In a hambulance.

How do you make a pair of shoes?

Get two shoes. Then you have a pair.

Where do eggplants come from?

Chickenplants.

If you gave one friend 15 cents and another friend a dime, what time would it be?

A quarter to two.

David: I dreamt I was eating a giant marshmallow.

Nathan: What happened?

David: When I woke up, my pillow was gone!

Why aren't dogs considered good dancers?

They have two left feet.

Where does a rat go when it has a toothache?

To the rodent-ist.

How many letters are in the alphabet?

There are eleven letters in "the alphabet."

Why did the cookie cry?

Because its parent was a wafer so long!

What is a really sad strawberry called?

A blueberry!

What does a toad say when they can't remember something?

"Oh no, I froggot."

What kind of keys are sweet and delicious?

Cookies!

Frank: I have two coins equaling fifteen cents. One of them is not a nickel. What are the two coins?

Kevin: I give up . . . what?

Frank: A dime and a nickel. One of the coins is not a nickel, but the other one is.

Brain-Busting Belly Laughs

Where do young cows eat lunch?

In the calf-eteria.

Which button cannot be unbuttoned?

Your belly button.

What kind of train has a head cold?

Achoo-achoo train.

Which aunt does a penguin like best?

Aunt Arctica.

Imagine you're trapped in a room behind a locked door. What's the best way to get out?

Stop imagining.

What did the beaver say to the tree?

It's been nice gnawing you.

What city are you in if you drop your waffle on the beach?

Sandy Eggo.

If two kids share six pieces of cherry pie, and one kid only gets to eat one piece, what does the other kid get?

A stomachache.

Jokes with Many Letters of the Alphabet in Them

Why did the phone walk into the water?

It was wading for a call.

Do eye shadow and lipstick ever argue?

Sometimes, but then they make up.

Why was the sailor sitting on a pack of playing cards?

Someone told them to sit on the deck.

What color is the wind?

Blew.

Which bathroom fixture would make a terrible life preserver?

The sink.

What's very easy to lift but very hard to throw?

A feather.

What four-letter word spells the same thing forward, backward, and upside down?

NOON

What should you use if you want to catch a school of fish?

A bookworm.

Try Not to LoL Challenge

And now for an important piece of joke-related information: The funny bone in your elbow isn't actually a bone at all. It's a nerve, and it's (incorrectly) called the "funny bone" because it feels funny if you happen to bump it. Now you know. And oh, by the way, try not to laugh with your mouth or your funny bone at the next twelve jokes.

Dennis: Can you name a city without any residents?

Corey: Yes—electri-city!

Who's a golfer's favorite wizard?

Harry Putter.

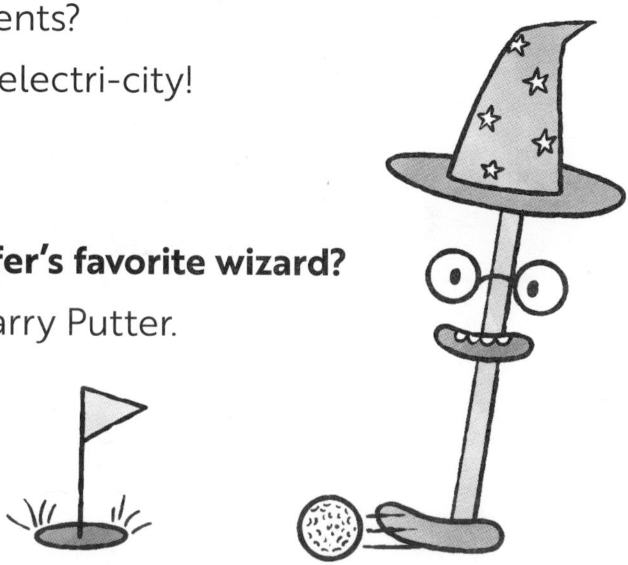

Why did the ram run off the cliff?

It didn't see the ewe turn.

Which days are the strongest?

Saturday and Sunday.

The others are weak-days.

What is something that needs to be taken before you can have it?

Your picture.

What do dogs and phones have in common?

Both have collar ID.

Why should you never brush your teeth with your left hand?

Because a toothbrush works better.

What do you call a beehive without an exit?

Un-bee-leaveable.

What do you call a fish with two knees?

A "two-knee" fish.

Why couldn't the bad sailor learn the alphabet?

Because they always got lost at C.

What's the best thing about Switzerland?

I don't know, but the flag is a big plus!

What has a spine but no bones?

A book.

Prank You Very Much

Here's a prank one of my kids did to me. You might want to do it if and when the situation is right. But if that's not possible, don't try it . . . and just laugh at what my kid did.

My son took a screenshot of my computer desktop, then left that image open on my screen. It looked as if my computer was totally frozen. The cursor wouldn't move. The menus wouldn't open. I was frustrated for a moment, until he laughed and told me what he'd done.

By the way—successful pranking always depends on doing it at the right time, and not letting the joke go on too long. For example, if my son had pranked me when I had an important project to finish and it kept me from using my computer . . . not so funny. And if he'd waited until I'd called a repairperson . . . well, that wouldn't have been funny at all.

Remember that anytime you're joking around, timing is crucial.

CAN YOU DIG-IT?

Here's an easy way to multiply any two-digit number by 11 . . .

Just add the two digits together and place the sum between the original two digits. Like this:

Let's say you want to multiply 34 by 11. Just add the 3 and the 4 (that's 7), and place the 7 between the 3 and the 4. Your total (and the right answer) is 374. Check it out . . . 34 x 11 is indeed 374.

Let's try that again with 51 x 11.

5 + 1 = 6. Put that 6 in between the 5 and the 1, and your answer is 561.

By the way, if the two digits you're adding have a total of more than 10, you increase the original first digit by one and put the second number from the total in between. Like this . . .

68 x 11. The total of 6 + 8 is 14. So you add one to the 6 (making it 7) and then put the 4 between the 7 and the 8. And so, 68 X 11 = 748.

And so on.

Of course, you're not often asked to multiply two-digit numbers by 11, but if you ever are, you'll surely know how!

Jokes My Kids Have Told Me

My kids and I often share jokes at bedtime. Here are some of the best ones they've told me over the years . . .

What do sea monsters eat?

Fish and ships.

What is the shortest month of the year?

May—it only has three letters.

Anne Marie: Want to hear a joke about bowling?

Sofia: Spare me!

Speaking of bowling, what kind of cats like to go bowling?

Alley cats.

How do moths swim?

They do the butterfly stroke.

What happens when ice cream gets angry?

It has a meltdown.

Alex: My neighbor slept under their car last night.

Annie: Why?

Alex: They wanted to wake up oily.

What do you call a pile of cats?

A *meow*-ntain.

Where's the one place you should never take your dog?

To a flea market.

Speaking of dogs, what is a dog's favorite breakfast meal?

Pooched eggs.

What says, "Quick, quick"?

A duck with hiccups.

Why was the pirate able to buy a ship for only one dollar?

It was on sail.

What do you call a snake that loves building houses?

A boa constructor.

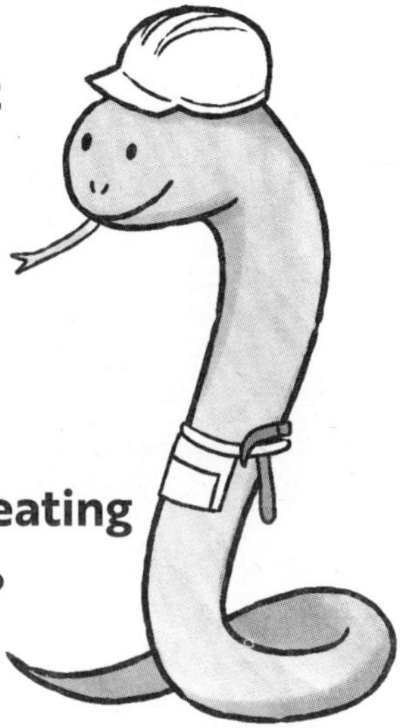

What do ghosts enjoy eating when it's hot out?

I scream.

Where is the best place in school to grow flowers?

Kinder-garden!

What do you call a penguin in the White House?

Lost.

It's Time to Turn on the Tee-Hee

What do you call a dog that can do magic?

A Labracadabrador.

How do you get a good price on a sled?

You have toboggan.

April: Look at that baby snake!

Jayde: How do you know it's a baby?

April: I can tell by the rattle.

What kind of car does an egg drive?

A Yolkswagen.

Why did the astronaut move to a bigger house?

They wanted more space.

Why was the envelope late for the party?

It took a long time to get addressed.

How does a mosquito get from place to place?

It itch-hikes!

What do you call young avocados?

Avo-kiddos!

Did you hear about the person who was afraid of hurdles?

They got over it.

What has five toes and isn't your foot?

My foot.

Ellie: Dr. Wilson, my pet pig has a rash.

Dr. Wilson: Here—use this . . .

Ellie: What is it?

Dr. Wilson: An oinkment!

How do mice floss their teeth?

They use string cheese.

Speaking of twins, what fruit do twins like best?

Pears.

What day of the week is a good one for twins to be born?

Twos-day!

Elizabeth: Does your dog bite?

Randy: Never.

Elizabeth: Then how do you feed him?

How do you make your soup golden?

Add 24 carrots.

Why aren't pigs good drivers?

They always hog the road.

How did the barber win the race?

They knew a shortcut.

What's a good book to read if you want to learn about chickens?

The hencyclopedia!

Shelly: It took 20 workers 10 days to build a house. How many days would it take for 10 workers to build the same house?

Wayne: Absolutely no time at all—it's already built!

What flavor of ice cream is never early?

Choco-late.

Why did the baseball player get in trouble?

They stole second base.

What's a planet's favorite thing to read?

Comet books!

Where does Friday come before Thursday?

In the dictionary.

Jokes to Tell on Tuesdays at 4:08 p.m. (or Anytime)

What ten-letter word starts with GAS?

Automobile.

What will you always find at the end of a rainbow?

The letter *w*.

What kind of ears do engines have?

Engineers.

What do you call a large furry animal that's caught in the rain?

A drizzly bear.

What has eighteen legs and catches flies?

A baseball team.

What kind of room doesn't have any doors, windows, or walls?

A mushroom.

If you throw a white stone into the Red Sea, what will it become?

Wet.

What do you call it when a T. rex makes a goal in soccer?

A dino-score.

What do you call a bee that's always complaining?

A grumblebee.

How does a shell get from place to place in the ocean?

It takes a taxicrab.

Kevin: I know a person who hasn't slept in twenty days.

Scott: That seems impossible!

Kevin: Not at all—they sleep at night.

What kind of music do balloons dislike?

Pop music.

Why is a moon rock tastier than an Earth rock?

Because it's a little meteor.

How do you say goodbye to boiling water?

"So long, you will be mist!"

What has two legs but never walks?

A pair of pants.

Hotel clerk: The room costs $100 a night. But it's $25 if you make your own bed.

Guest: Fine. I'll make my own bed.

Hotel clerk: Okay. Wait here; I'll get you some wood, nails, and a hammer.

By the Way . . .

Do you know what's just as hard as writing and compiling jokes for you to laugh at (or sometimes, for you to try not to laugh at)?

Coming up with category headings for the jokes.

Oh sure, you saw the spooky jokes with the heading "Boo to You!" . . . and you probably read right past it to get to the funny stuff. Right?

I'm sure that's the case.

But think about this—before I put that punny heading on those jokes, I took a lot of time to come up with other possibilities, like . . .

Witch Jokes Do You Like Best?

These Jokes Will Haunt You!

Some Spook-tacular Jokes for You!

Will You Like These Jokes? I Couldn't Scare Less!

Jokes Just Right for Goblin!

Howl-oween Ha-Ha's!

And even . . .

Trick or Treat, Smell My Feet, I Think These Jokes Are Hard to Beat!

I hope you think I chose the right category heading. But coming up with the others was a great exercise in creativity. And here's how I did it—I made a list of Halloween-themed words. Then I tried to think of a pun that would use each of the words in a clever way.

Of course, not every project calls for a punny line. But when you have to title something and want to be clever, ask yourself, What do I know about that subject? Which words are related? Write down those words, then try to come up with appropriate puns. Can you do it? Absolutely! Will you have as much fun as I did making the list of Halloween puns?

Oh my gourdness . . . yes!

Try These in Your Stand-Up Comedy Act

You—yes, you—could have a career as a comedian. Memorize some of the following jokes, and get ready to see your name in lights on a big theater marquee! (Or even if you just tell them in a school talent show, that'd be awesome.)

How do cows stay up to date?

They read the *moo*-spaper.

My boat is sick. Where should I take it?

To the dock, of course.

What do you get when you put a car and a pet together?

A carpet.

How much money does a skunk have?

Just one scent.

What kind of pie can fly?

A magpie.

Why do hamburgers go south for the winter?

So they don't freeze their buns off.

Why did the bird go to the hospital?

It needed some medical tweetment.

How did the lettuce win the race?

It got a head start.

What swims and starts with the letter *T*?

Three ducks.

Kamal: I'm very good at sleeping.
Evander: How good?
Kamal: I can do it with my eyes closed!

Why did the cantaloupe jump into the lake?

It wanted to be a watermelon.

Elliot: Guess what I saw today.

William: What?

Elliot: Everything I looked at!

How long does it take to make butter?

An e-churn-ity.

What do you call a sleeping bull?

A bulldozer.

What's the first thing Santa's elves learn in school?

The elf-abet.

What do you call a line of people waiting to get haircuts?

A barber-queue.

Luna: A slice of apple pie is $2.00 in Jamaica and $3.00 in the Bahamas.

Mollie: Why are you telling me that?

Luna: Those are the pie rates of the Caribbean.

Why did everyone enjoy being around the volcano?

It's just so lava-ble.

Speaking of volcanoes, where do they go to wash their hands?

The lava-tory!

When is a door sweet and tasty?

When it's jammed!

How do you make a bandstand?

Take away their chairs.

Why can you never surprise mountains?

They peak.

What do you get if you cross an angry sheep with a moody cow?

An animal that's in a baaaaaaaaad moooooooood.

Knock, knock.

Who's there?

Closure.

Closure who?

Closure mouth when you're eating!

Why are snails bad at racing?

They're sluggish.

Lucy: I used to a have job collecting leaves.

George: Did you make any money?

Lucy: I was raking it in!

How do you stop a baby from spilling food on the table?

Feed them on the floor!

Why is Peter Pan always flying?

Because he can never neverland.

Which rock group has four members who don't sing?

Mount Rushmore.

Found and Lost

I have two siblings. Sometimes one is weird, and sometimes the other one is weird. But they're almost never weird at the same time, which, if you think about it, is pretty weird.

Anyway, yesterday my sister came home from school and, as usual, ran to the piano. And she was standing up the whole time. I finally said, "Jenna, sit down when you're playing." And she said, "I can't—I'm practicing 'The Star-Spangled Banner'!"

Like I said, weird.

And this afternoon, my younger brother, Andrew, started digging in the backyard. Our parents have bought him every kind of shovel and scraper and digger you can imagine, but for some reason he prefers to use the ice cream scooper.

But wait, that's not the weird part.

Somehow he dug a hole that was about five feet down—so deep that if he fell in we'd probably have to call the emergency squad or big, strong Mr. Morris next door to pull him out. (Mr. Morris is the person who tugged our family car out of a big snowbank last year, with my parents still in it.)

Anyway, while Andrew was digging and digging, I suddenly heard, "Heyowmiffc'mere!"—which is what "Hey, wow, Mitch, come here" sounds like through a retainer.

I dropped my salami-and-marshmallow after-school snack sandwich and ran to help the kid, which is what big siblings do. And would you believe Andrew had unearthed an actual, authentic, original, priceless artifact from hundreds or even thousands of years ago!

It was a broken slab of rock about the size of Andrew's head—with the word *KING* carved into it! Cool, huh? I mean, living right here in our backyard was a famous, legendary king from the olden days! I knew we were going to be instant millionaires—Andrew for finding the slab, and me for what I said next . . .

"Let's dig more; there's probably a whole kingdom under there!"

Andrew agreed, and we both pounced on the dirt, looking for even more riches. Andrew suggested inviting Jenna to help, but she was busy playing piano. Besides, I was already planning to give Andrew 10 percent of my newfound fortune; why should I have to split it any further?

We dug and dug, and we were soon covered with dirt and mud. And then . . .

Andrew yanked another rock slab out of the dirt! It said *PAR*!

We put the pieces together to spell *KING PAR*. Hey, I thought maybe he was a ruler in the sixteenth century. He ruled France. Or Spain. Or New Zealand. Or Texas. Anyway, the story was growing, so . . .

We covered the ground with the largest blanket we could find (from our parents' bed) and ran to do an internet search on King Par.

Nothing.

Dad's right about the internet—you can never get the information you need. How could there be nothing about the famous King Par who lived on our property in the sixteenth century?

(Of course, if you're wondering how he could've ruled France or Spain or places like that while living in our backyard in Kansas, so was I. But then I realized that it was long ago, and he was so mighty, it was totally possible.)

Anyway . . . with no information to be found, we went back and dug further. And sure enough, a little while later . . .

Another piece! A tiny slab of rock that said *NO*.

We laid the pieces together and realized . . .

Aha! It wasn't KING PAR! It was KING PAR NO!

We left the pieces right there, covered the dirt with the blanket (man, our folks are gonna need to wash that!) . . . and ran back to the computer.

KING PARNO. KING PARNO. Search results about this great leader . . .

Nothing.

Andrew had a brilliant idea. Maybe it was KING NOPAR.

We checked. We struck out.

Too tired to dig, we decided to go get the slabs and hide them in Andrew's room . . . then pick up the project tomorrow.

Just then, Jenna called to us from the backyard . . .

"Hey, guys, who broke the sign?"

Andrew yelled back, "What sign, Jenna?"

"This one," she shouted back. "The one that says 'NO PARKING.'"

Like I said, weird.

A Final Word from Alan Katz

Okay, that's it for the funny stuff.

I hope you'll share jokes every day, and laugh a lot... but remember, jokes are only funny if *everyone* can enjoy them! Jokes that make fun of other people are never acceptable. Kindness always comes first!

Keep laughing!

Bye!

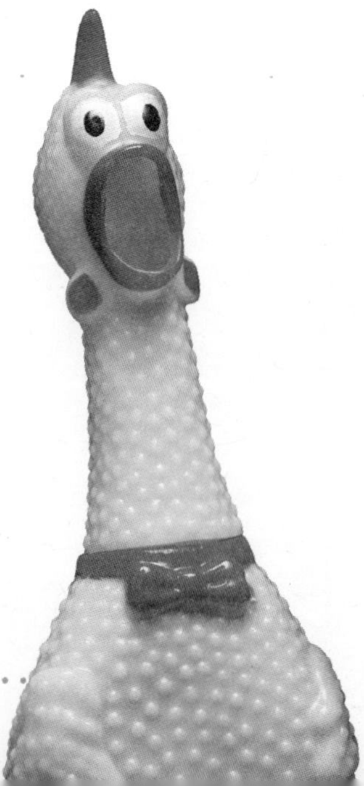